D1636631

THE MOTHERS' ROSARY

PAULA CAPPS

MATER PRESS   ST. LOUIS

ACKNOWLEDGMENTS

The Catholic Edition of the Revised Standard Version of the Bible, copyright 1965, 1966 by the Division of Christian Education of the National Council of the Churches of Christ in the United States of America. Used by permission. All rights reserved.

Unless otherwise noted, all images contained in this book including the cover are from the Villa Duchesne and Oak Hill School chapel (Michael Jacobs Photography).

Imprimatur: †Most Reverend Robert J. Carlson
Archbishop of St. Louis
September 26, 2016

In accordance with Canon 827, permission to publish has been granted on September 26, 2016, by the Most Reverend Robert J. Carlson, Archbishop, Archdiocese of St. Louis. Permission to publish is an indication that nothing contrary to Church teaching is contained in this work. It does not imply any endorsement of the opinions expressed in the publication; nor is any liability assumed by this permission.

DEDICATION

TO MY FAMILY

I dedicate this book to my loving husband, Tom, and our children, George, Tom, Charlie, Kenny, James, Polly, Matthew and Mary Therese. The Lord has truly blessed me! Through them, God has revealed His love and given me a glimpse of His Heavenly Kingdom.

TO ALL MOTHERS

"The most important person on earth is a mother. She cannot claim the honor of having built Notre Dame Cathedral. She need not. She has built something more magnificent than any cathedral – a dwelling for an immortal soul, the tiny perfection of her baby's body.... The angels have not been blessed with such a grace. They cannot share in God's creative miracle to bring new saints to Heaven. Only a human mother can. Mothers are closer to God the Creator than any other creature. God joins forces with mothers in performing this act of creation.... What on God's good earth is more glorious than this: to be a mother?"

-Joseph Cardinal Mindszenty

IN HER HONOR

In celebration of the 200th-year anniversary of St. Rose Philippine Duchesne's voyage to America in 1818, this book is in her honor. May we learn from her simple trust in God as revealed in her own words: "I am where God wills me to be, and so I have found rest and security. God's wisdom governs me, God's power defends me, God's mercy encompasses me, God's joy sustains me and all will go well with me."

Contents

FOREWORD

In her Introduction, my wife tells you how she started a weekly Mothers' Rosary with my sister at our children's school over twenty years ago, shortly before giving birth to our fifth child. What Polly doesn't tell you is how faithful she was in showing up, week after week, to lead the rosary for the next 20 years. We would eventually be blessed with eight children and, as you can imagine, there were many times over those 20 years when it would have been much easier for her to find an excuse not to go. Yet, even if she had been up most of the night feeding a newborn or tending to a sick child, she would somehow manage to get everyone up, dressed, fed and where they were supposed to be, and still be there to lead the rosary every week at 8 A.M. Her devotion to her children and the school and her unwavering confidence in the Blessed Mother's intercession for them made this weekly commitment a mission of love.

Her perseverance, and that of the loyal band of mothers who joined her in prayer, has been abundantly rewarded. I have seen how the entire school community has been enriched in so many ways from the graces and blessings received through the devotion of those faithful mothers. A mother's intercession is so powerful and the Blessed Mother's is the most powerful of all; imagine, then, how powerful the intercessory prayers of a group of mothers calling upon the intercession of the Blessed Mother must be.

Everyone can profit from the meditations contained in this book, but they are particularly directed to mothers. They are written from a mother's heart and are inspired by the love of Mary for her Divine Son and for us all. I marvel at the depth of Polly's insights into the holy vocation of motherhood. In the words of Pope St. John Paul II, "the family is ... the heart of the civilization of love." And, as every husband and father knows, the mother is the heart of the family. Mothers are channels of God's grace to their husbands and children, and they uniquely imitate Christ and His Blessed Mother through their day-in, day-out self-sacrificing love for their families. Mothers give themselves utterly and completely to their families, subordinating their own desires and wills to the desires and needs of their spouse and children. This self-sacrifice is often (if not always) unheralded, unrecognized and underappreciated. But it is extraordinarily powerful in building strong, happy, holy families. What better model for a self-sacrificing, loving, fruitful mother could there be than Mary, the Mother of God and the Mother of us all? And what better way is there to become a holy wife and mother than by meditating upon and imitating the love between Mary and her Divine Son?

I have been blessed beyond measure to have met and married Polly. She is a wellspring of joy and inspiration to me and an extraordinary mother to our children. She has made each of us a better person through her goodness and unending love, sacrifice and devotion. She has truly made the path to Heaven easier for her spouse and children. It is my hope that every wife and mother who uses this book becomes more like the Blessed Mother and as much a blessing and source of grace and inspiration to their families as my wife has been to ours.

Finally, in closing, I want to tell all those who have participated in the Mothers' Rosary through the years how grateful Polly is to each and every one of you. Mothers have come and gone as their children have entered and left the school, but she feels an everlasting bond with all of you.

Thomas H. Capps
January 1, 2016
Solemnity of Mary, Mother of God

INTRODUCTION

In January 1994, I was well into my third trimester of pregnancy; in fact, I was due to deliver my fifth child in two weeks. My sister-in-law, Mary Jo, and I decided to start a prayer group at Villa Duchesne and Oak Hill School, the school that our children attended. The plan was to gather a group of mothers in the school's beautiful chapel once a week and pray the rosary. The prayer group soon became known as the "Mothers' Rosary."

I knew the timing wasn't ideal, but Mary Jo and I had been talking about doing it for a while and it became apparent to me that we just needed to "do it." Besides, I noticed that whenever I had the intention or idea to do something worthwhile or good, my mind became immediately inundated with all the reasons or excuses why I should refrain from proceeding. The phrase, "the road to hell is lined with good intentions," began to overcome all those "reasonable excuses." So I felt that I just had to start or I may never do it. Even though the timing seemed all wrong I figured I needed to take that small leap of faith. "Trust in God and just do it anyway," I told myself.

I have found that such "leaps of faith," no matter how small, are always rewarded. I am reminded of the words of a holy priest that my husband had as a confessor many years ago. This priest had stressed to my husband the importance of praying the family rosary every night at home. My husband tried to explain to the priest that it would be more than difficult as we had several small children with little to no attention span. This did not deter the priest in the least from his pestering. "Do it anyway," he commanded. We did. It was chaotic. But we persevered and it was fruitful. To this day my young adult children can be found with rosaries in their pockets, an example that showed me that "leaps of faith," even small ones, never go unnoticed by our loving Father.

So even though it was smack in the middle of the school year and I would soon be busy with a newborn, we asked and received permission from the administration and then began to spread the word to the school community. I still recall wondering to myself, "Will anyone come?" I don't remember the exact number that showed up for the first rosary, but we probably had about ten mothers join us in the Villa Duchesne and Oak Hill School chapel at 8:00 on a Tuesday morning. Mary Jo had the wonderful idea of asking Mother Mary Gray McNally, RSCJ, to lead our first Mothers' Rosary. Mother McNally died a few years later, but I still feel her presence and her blessing even now as we gather more than twenty years later to continue to pray for our children, their teachers and the entire school community.

Starting a rosary group at my children's school has brought many blessings. I believe it has solicited the aid of the Blessed Mother to protect my children and all the children of Villa Duchesne and Oak Hill School. In addition, I have witnessed how it has enriched the community. It has brought together teachers, administrators and parents in prayer as we petition and pray for each other's intentions. Sometimes we have only a few mothers; other times we have many. We've been joined by a whole classroom of children, a large group of parents who came to pray for a fellow parent who was undergoing serious surgery, heads of school, religious, alumnae, teachers and staff.

Mothers come with their pre-school children who are sometimes still dressed in "jammies." I will always remember one precious image of a mother sitting cross legged against the wall of the chapel with her toddler on her lap drinking from a bottle and the rosary wrapped around the hands of both the mother and her baby. I fumbled with my phone to quickly take a picture, but I was too late; the baby moved and the moment was gone. It was a moment meant only for my memory. "Baby noises" are most welcome and put everyone at ease as they remind us of who we are and what we are doing there.

Most importantly, mothers come to pray to the mother of us all, Mary, the mother of our Lord and Savior, who, through the action of the Holy Spirit, gave Jesus His humanity and then at the foot of the cross, through the action of Jesus, became our mother. We come to ask her to help us fulfill our incredibly awesome vocation of motherhood and to help us stay close to her Son. Mary mothered the Son of God perfectly; therefore, no one knows better than Mary what we need to do as mothers to succeed in raising our children to become all that God intends for them to become, holy men and women.

Our children face so many challenges, so many negative spiritual attacks. They need our prayers! We need to pray so that we can guide and strengthen them. In addition, the teachers and staff that spend so much of the day with our children need our prayers. A rosary prayed from a mother's heart for her children is a prayer that is one with the Immaculate Heart of Mary and therefore extremely powerful. It will always be heard.

Indeed, the blessings from the Mothers' Rosary are many, and I believe they are far greater than we can realize here on earth. Mary Jo stated it nicely when she said, "Spiritual works of mercy often do not have the immediate gratifying results that corporal works of mercy do, as prayers are being answered outside our awareness." The belief that our prayers are effective requires faith. And it is faith that brings us to trust *our Lord*, not ourselves, to have everything already worked out for the best. We pray not to change God's plan but rather that the will of the Father might be more fully carried out in us and in our children. As a result, we find peace in trusting that our Mother and her Son will always take care of us.

While our prayer group began with and continues to pray the rosary, other devotions with meditations and reflections written to focus the hearts of mothers on the perfect motherhood of the Blessed Virgin Mary have been added over time and are included in this book. Finally, I have provided a small collection of favorite prayers that I have come across, or that have been given to me, over the years. It is my intention and sincere hope that this book will be used by mothers to help them pray for their children, whether in a group at their children's school or in the privacy of their own homes. The spiritual benefits and rewards are assured.

THE SCHOOL

Since we seek to partner with the teachers and staff in promoting the positive formation of our children, our prayer group offers prayers not only for our children but also for the whole school community. As members of that community, we naturally contribute to and build on the school's heritage, traditions and even the prayers of those who went before us. Therefore, our prayer group incorporates the traditions special to our children's school and petitions the school's patron saints to be our ultimate prayer warriors.

My children attended Villa Duchesne and Oak Hill School in St. Louis, Missouri. It is a Sacred Heart school founded by the Religious of the Sacred Heart, an order whose roots began in 1800 in France and whose foundress was St. Madeleine Sophie Barat. St. Rose Philippine Duchesne, who became one of the first religious of the Society, traveled to the United States in 1818 to open a school in the New World. Villa Duchesne opened its doors in 1929 and is named for this pioneering saint.

Embedded in the history and tradition of the Society of the Sacred Heart, Mary has been especially loved and honored under the titles, Mater Admirabilis, the Immaculate Heart of Mary, and Our Lady of Sorrows. In keeping with this tradition, our prayer group honors Our Blessed Mother under these titles when we pray the rosary, the Stations of the Cross, and the Rosary of the Seven Sorrows of Mary.

Endearingly special to and patroness of all Sacred Heart schools, Mater Admirabilis is Latin for "Mother Most Admirable." Either a statue or another image of the beautiful Mater can be found in every Sacred Heart school. Therefore, when we gather to pray in the school chapel, our prayer group offers our rosary through the intercession of Mater. During Lent, in addition to the recitation of the weekly rosary, our prayer group prays the Stations of the Cross through the eyes of Mary. It is through this devotion that we as mothers unite our hearts in a special way to the

 Immaculate Heart of Mary, who most perfectly united her heart to her Son's as she walked with Him on the road to Calvary and watched Him suffer and die for the world. The original seal of the Society of the Sacred Heart depicts the union of the Immaculate Heart of Mary and the Sacred Heart of Jesus. It is my hope that this variation of the Stations of the Cross, *A Mother's Walk With Her Son*, will reveal the union of the Immaculate Heart of Mary with the Sacred Heart of Jesus.

Finally, the devotion of the Rosary of the Seven Sorrows of Mary is steeped in the tradition of the Sacred Heart since St. Madeleine Sophie frequently turned to Our Lady of Sorrows, especially in times of great need. In the Villa Duchesne and Oak Hill School chapel there is a beautiful side altar dedicated to Our Lady of Sorrows. The Feast of Our Lady of Sorrows is September 15th and is celebrated in the school with a liturgy. Our prayer group prays the Rosary of the Seven Sorrows of Mary during the week of September 15th and during Advent.

While the meditations and prayers herein reflect the heritage and traditions upon which the school that my children attended was founded, it is very much encouraged that the saints and patrons special to you, your family, and your school be added to enrich and personalize your prayer life and group. Doing so will not only help you to become familiar with the heritage of the faith family that surrounds you but will also draw you into a deeper relationship with all those brothers and sisters who are saints reigning with our Lord, perfectly united to Christ in Heaven and yearning to become a part of your life. It is in this way that we enter into and celebrate the beautiful and varied richness of our glorious Church.

Mater Admirabilis in the Trinità dei Monti in Rome

MATER ADMIRABILIS

Mater Admirabilis, Mother Most Admirable, is the title of what is widely considered one of the most beautiful depictions of our Blessed Mother. Originally a fresco painted in 1844 on the wall of the Trinità dei Monti, a Sacred Heart convent and school in Rome, the painting was accorded its striking title by Pope Pius IX in 1846. The artist, Pauline Perdrau, a Sacred Heart postulant at the time, claimed to have felt the presence of the Blessed Mother while working continuously for 13 hours on her face. Today, the Blessed Mother under the title of "Mater Admirabilis" is celebrated as a feast day in every Sacred Heart school around the world on October 20th.

St. Madeleine Sophie once said, "We must know how to inspire in our pupils a passion for the beautiful." This painting, I believe, is emblematic of how the mission of the Society of the Sacred Heart has always been clothed in exceptional, remarkable beauty. Villa Duchesne and Oak Hill School has been built upon the beautiful, rich traditions envisioned by St. Madeleine Sophie. These traditions are carefully woven into a distinctly Catholic education which is drawn directly from the Heart of Christ. The words of Mother Rosalie Hill, RSCJ, serve as an apt description of the totality of a Sacred Heart education: "Beauty will attract them, but truth will hold them."

Rosary Prayers

The leader is responsible for beginning each prayer followed by recitation of the **bold italics** by all.

SIGN OF THE CROSS (As children of God, we do all in His name.)

In the name of the Father, and of the Son, and of the Holy Spirit. Amen. *(As you say this, with your right hand touch your forehead when you say* Father, *touch your breastbone when you say* Son, *touch your left shoulder when you say* Holy, *and touch your right shoulder when you say* Spirit.*)*

OPENING PRAYER (To be prayed by the leader)

WE OFFER THIS ROSARY for our children and all the children of this school. We pray to Mater that she may guide us in our endeavor to be good, loving mothers, and that we may do our best to raise these children of God according to His will – so they may grow to be holy men and women, seeking only to fulfill a Christian life here on earth according to the example of our Lord Jesus Christ. We also pray that whatever vocation they pursue in this life will be filled in loving service to our Lord and will only lead them closer to their ultimate home in Heaven. We ask that the Holy Spirit guide and strengthen the faculty, staff and religious of this community who play such a critical role in nurturing and teaching our children. We pray dear Blessed Mother that our children remain pure and open of heart so that they may grow to know God's holy will for them here on earth, that they may stay true to His Holy Catholic Church, and that they may be strengthened by the Holy Spirit to have the courage to carry out that will. And for all those who have asked for our prayers, we pray especially for (mention any intercessory prayers) and for our own special intentions.

THE APOSTLES' CREED

I BELIEVE IN GOD, the Father Almighty, Creator of Heaven and earth; and in Jesus Christ, His only Son, our Lord, Who was conceived by the Holy Spirit, born of the Virgin Mary, suffered under Pontius Pilate, was crucified, died, and was buried. He descended into Hell; the third day He rose again from the dead; He ascended into Heaven, and sits at the right hand of God, the Father Almighty; from thence He shall come to judge the living and the dead. *I believe in the Holy Spirit, the Holy Catholic Church, the Communion of Saints, the forgiveness of sins, the resurrection of the body, and life everlasting. Amen.*

THE OUR FATHER

OUR FATHER, Who art in Heaven, hallowed be Thy Name. Thy kingdom come, Thy will be done on earth as it is in Heaven. *Give us this day our daily bread, and forgive us our trespasses, as we forgive those who trespass against us. And lead us not into temptation, but deliver us from evil. Amen.*

THE HAIL MARY

HAIL MARY, full of grace, the Lord is with thee. Blessed art thou among women, and blessed is the fruit of thy womb, Jesus. *Holy Mary, Mother of God, pray for us sinners, now and at the hour of our death. Amen.*

THE GLORY BE

GLORY BE to the Father, and to the Son, and to the Holy Spirit. *As it was in the beginning, is now, and ever shall be, world without end. Amen.*

THE FATIMA PRAYER

O MY JESUS, *forgive us our sins, save us from the fires of Hell, lead all souls to Heaven, especially those who are in most need of Thy mercy. Amen.*

HAIL HOLY QUEEN

HAIL HOLY QUEEN, *mother of mercy, our life, our sweetness, and our hope. To thee do we cry, poor banished children of Eve. To thee do we send up our sighs, mourning and weeping in this valley of tears. Turn, then, most gracious advocate, thine eyes of mercy toward us. And after this, our exile, show unto us the blessed fruit of thy womb, Jesus. O clement, O loving, O sweet Virgin Mary.*

Pray for us, O holy Mother of God, *that we may be made worthy of the promises of Christ. Amen.*

SAINT INVOCATION (We ask for the intercession of our school's patron saints.)

St. Rose Philippine Duchesne, *pray for us.*
St. Madeleine Sophie Barat, *pray for us.*

ST. MICHAEL THE ARCHANGEL PRAYER

ST. MICHAEL THE ARCHANGEL, *defend us in battle. Be our protection against the wickedness and snares of the Devil. May God rebuke him, we humbly pray, and do thou, O Prince of the heavenly hosts, by the power of God, thrust into hell Satan, and all the evil spirits, who prowl about the world seeking the ruin of souls. Amen.*

How To Pray The Rosary

1. Begin by making the *Sign of the Cross*. Say the *Opening Prayer*.

2. Holding the Crucifix, say the *Apostles' Creed*.

3. On the first large bead next to the Crucifix, say an *Our Father*.

4. Say three *Hail Marys,* one for each of the next three smaller beads, praying in turn before each *Hail Mary* for an increase in Faith, Hope and Charity.

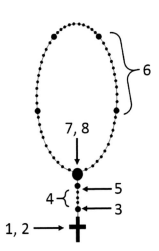

5. Say the *Glory Be*.

6. For each of the five decades, announce the mystery and read one of the corresponding meditation options. Then pray an *Our Father* (large bead), 10 *Hail Marys* (one for each of the ten smaller beads), followed by the *Glory Be* and the *Fatima prayer*.

7. When the five decades are completed, finish the rosary with the *Hail Holy Queen* prayer.

8. Other favorite prayers may be added at this point. We invoke the aid of St. Madeleine Sophie Barat and St. Rose Philippine Duchesne, knowing that they have a special love for our school. We ask them to "pray for us."

9. We conclude with the *St. Michael the Archangel* prayer. We recite this prayer for "peace in the world."

10. Finish by making the *Sign of the Cross*.

ROSARY MEDITATIONS

The following meditations are organized by mystery. Therefore, all the Joyful Mystery meditations are together, followed by the Luminous, Sorrowful, and finally the Glorious. Although our prayer group prays the rosary on the same day each week, we alternate the mysteries. When we began praying the rosary at our children's school we prayed on Tuesdays. The Sorrowful Mysteries are commonly prayed on Tuesdays. But if we prayed only Sorrowful Mysteries every week, it would be, as one mother noted, "very sorrowful." So we alternate the mysteries every week. We also cycle through the meditations for each mystery so that the meditations remain somewhat "fresh and new." The meditations are an important part of the rosary for that is where we encounter Christ as we contemplate His life and the life of His mother as revealed to us under the inspiration of the Holy Spirit in the Scriptures and the Tradition of the Church.

THE JOYFUL MYSTERIES

The Annunciation

- The angel Gabriel announces to Mary that she will bear the Son of God, if she agrees. Mary says "yes" to God and immediately God unites Himself to Mary's flesh and God becomes man. Mary, pray for us that we may always trust in God and say "yes" to all that He asks of us.

- "And Mary said, 'Behold, I am the handmaid of the Lord; let it be to me according to your word'" (Luke 1:38). We pray for our children that they may always be open to hearing God's will and be prompt in consenting to it.

- God provided His Son with a mother whose heart was full of grace, to love Him as He deserved to be loved. We need to enter into the mystery of Mary's Immaculate Heart so that we may learn to love Jesus with the Heart of Mary.

- Mary trusted God completely. In her humility she always allowed God to work in her life. Our children are a sign of God's power working through us. Mary, increase our appreciation for this creative action, which often requires a dying to self, a letting go, a painful laboring, a long preparation, a humbling acceptance that we are not in control. Help us realize how blessed we are to be working in cooperation with God as mothers.

- Thank you, Mary, for saying "yes" to God. We would have no salvation without your "yes." The angel Gabriel did not demand it of you but rather asked you to bear the Son of God. Likewise, God will never demand of us to do His will. It is always our choice – our destiny is determined by our response to God's call.

The Visitation

- Elizabeth rejoices in the knowledge that Mary is bearing the Son of God, the Redeemer of the world. She has been enlightened by the Holy Spirit and by the holy infant in her womb, John the Baptist. Holiness enables the Holy Spirit to move, inspire and speak in us. Teach us Mary how to be holy so that we may hear, recognize and understand the Holy Spirit Who is always ready and waiting to speak to us.

- We pray for our children that they will become less selfish and more generous in the service of others.

- Elizabeth and Mary rejoiced with each other over their God-given gift of motherhood. Give us the grace to always strive to acquire more humility and to grow in holiness so that we may realize and rediscover the immense blessing of motherhood, the blessing to bring forth and nourish new life. As Mary proclaimed in the Magnificat, we pray that we too may rejoice and marvel at God's holy work in us.

- Mary, within her first trimester of pregnancy, is hailed by her cousin Elizabeth as the "mother of my Lord." John the Baptist reacts to the presence of His Lord by leaping in the womb of Elizabeth. The Visitation calls to mind the immeasurable value of all human life from the moment of conception.

- At the Visitation, Mary praised God in the Magnificat. After receiving the Holy Eucharist, when we commune on the very Body, Blood, Soul and Divinity of Jesus, we closely image Our Lady as she carried Jesus in her womb. Help us Mary to realize this awesome reality and not only to prepare ourselves to receive Jesus worthily but also to spend the precious moments after receiving the Holy Eucharist praising and glorifying God as you did in the Magnificat.

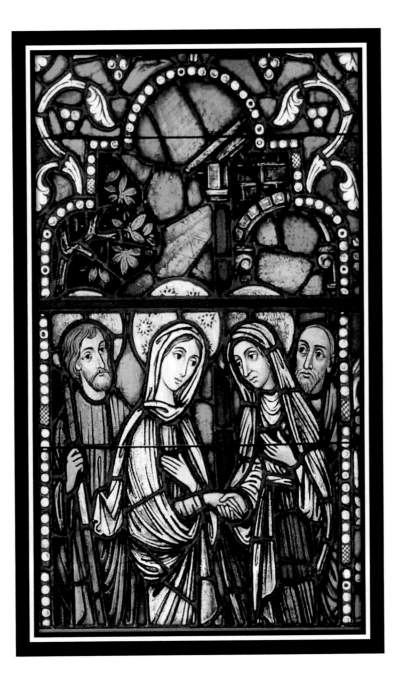

The Nativity

- Mary brings forth the Son of God into a world which is very far from perfect. Yet because of her perfect faith, her joy remains as she endures the hardships of the circumstances: her travel during the ninth month of her pregnancy on a donkey, her giving birth in a stable, having her privacy intruded on by shepherds and strangers, and her learning that there are those who seek to destroy her child. Help us Mary to endure our sufferings with the joy which comes from the knowledge and the faith that all is in God's hands.

- We pray for our children that they will live spiritually fruitful lives.

- As we strive to attain holiness through the channel of our spouse may we become ever more aware of God's love through the gift of the fruit of our marital love, our children. With each child may we become less selfish and more giving and thereby make room in our souls for more of God's love.

- What did Mary ponder as she held the Babe in her arms? Think of the first time we held our children. It is so easy to see the beauty of God in an infant. Mary, help us never to lose sight of the things that really matter in this life. Help us to keep our priorities straight, our eyes always focused on God, and help us not to become deceived by the comforts of this passing world.

- Christ enters the world through the love of a family. Jesus spent 30 of his 33 years here on earth in the privacy of the Holy Family, redeeming us through obedience, hard work, family prayer and all the ordinary daily chores, and thereby showing us that we are called to be saved through our ordinary activities and faithfully living out our vocations by raising up godly families.

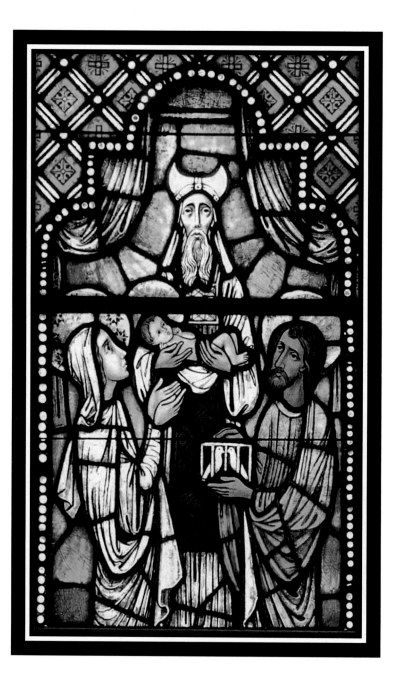

The Presentation of Jesus in the Temple

- Mary and Joseph present Jesus in the Temple in accordance with the Mosaic Law. They are faithful and obedient to every detail. Help us Mary to imitate you and Joseph as we raise our children so that we may pass on to them the precious gift of our faith in such a way that they will treasure it and pass it on with love to their children.

- When Jesus was presented in the Temple, Simeon prophesized that Mary would incur great suffering. However, she did not falter in performing her mission as co-redeemer of the world. We know that suffering is a part of this life here on earth. Help us Mary to accept all our sufferings with patience and love, especially those which involve our children.

- Even though Mary held the very Son of God in her arms, she humbly submitted to and obeyed the Law of Moses as she presented Jesus in the Temple. Help us Mary to teach our children the importance of obedience to and respect for their elders, parents, and teachers, but most of all God and His Holy Law which is preserved by His Church.

- We pray for our children that they may always remain faithful to the teachings of the Catholic Church.

- When Mary and Joseph took Jesus to the Temple for the presentation, holy Simeon and Anna were there praying for the opportunity to behold the promised Messiah. They patiently waited, perhaps years, praying and fasting. And finally they were rewarded for their faith and immediately recognized the infant Jesus as their Savior. Help us Mary to utilize the gift of prayer throughout our life so that we may always recognize our Lord.

The Finding of the Child Jesus in the Temple

- Jesus remained behind in the Temple, following His Father's will. It was also the will of God that Mary and Joseph should be searching for Jesus for three days. It was surely a panic-filled three days but it was necessary as God fulfilled His plan. Help us Mary to see the bigger picture when we are weighted down with sufferings. Help us not to despair, but to persevere in the faith that guarantees that Jesus will be there at the end of our search.

- "After three days they found him in the temple, sitting among the teachers, listening to them and asking them questions; and all who heard him were amazed at his understanding and his answers" (Luke 2:46-47). We pray for our children that they will grow to love the Holy Scriptures more and more every day.

- Jesus is found discussing the Holy Scriptures with the Jewish rabbis. Mary help us instill in our children a love for God's Holy Word. Help us to imitate you, so that by knowing and understanding God's saving plan for all mankind, we may enter into a deeper relationship with our Lord and increase our appreciation for His immense love for us.

- Jesus teaches us that God is our one true Father and that He should always come first in our lives. If we encourage and teach our children to love and obey God and His laws, they will then love and obey us, their parents.

- After being separated from Him for three days, Mary and Joseph found the child Jesus in the Temple doing the will of God. Mother Mary, if we or our children ever stray from the path leading home to Heaven or get lost, seek us out and bring us back into the safety of your motherly care. And at the end of our earthly life, we pray, dear Blessed Mother, that you find us, as you did Jesus, doing the will of the Father.

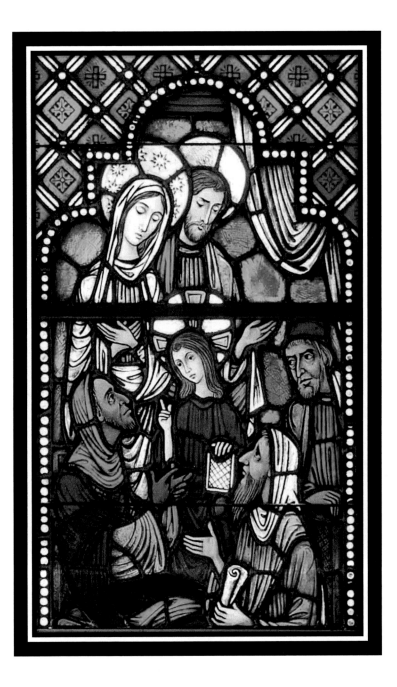

THE LUMINOUS MYSTERIES

Baptism of Jesus in the Jordan River

- "And when Jesus was baptized, he went up immediately from the water, and behold, the heavens were opened and he saw the Spirit of God descending like a dove, and alighting on him; and lo, a voice from heaven, saying, 'This is my beloved Son, with whom I am well pleased'" (Matthew 3:16-17). We may not hear God's voice or see the Spirit descending like a dove when an individual is baptized; however, rising from the font, every person truly becomes a child of God. Help us Blessed Mother to look on every person as a child of God and to treat them as you treated your Son, Jesus.
- We pray for our children that they may live out their baptismal vows every day as true children of God.
- John baptizes in the river Jordan, the very river the Israelites crossed to go from slavery and the wilderness to freedom and the Promised Land. Jesus now consecrates those waters by His baptism, transforming those who are now baptized in His name into children of God, and divinizing the journey we now must take to cross over into the true Promised Land.
- Jesus humbles Himself and asks to be baptized by John. John's baptism of repentance was to ready the Jewish people for the New Covenant in Christ. Jesus had no need of it and yet insisted that it be done so that others would follow His example. Often examples are the most effective ways of teaching. Help us Mary to humble ourselves so that our actions may become good examples for our children to follow.
- We pray for the teachers of our children that they may give our children an appreciation and fervent love for their faith.

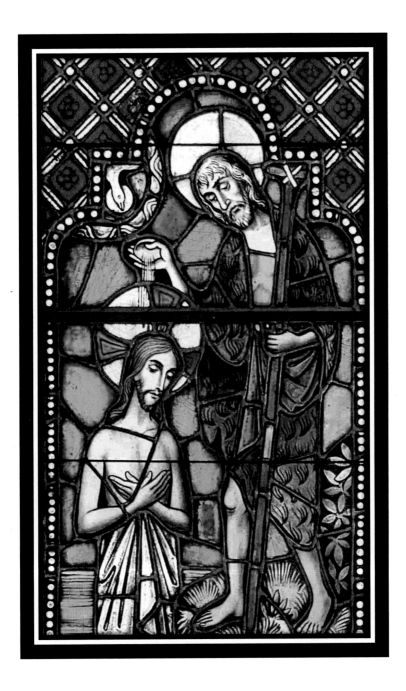

The Wedding Feast at Cana

- "When the wine failed, the mother of Jesus said to him, 'They have no wine.' And Jesus said to her, 'O woman, what have you to do with me? My hour has not yet come.' His mother said to the servants, 'Do whatever he tells you'" (John 2:3-5). It is at Mary's request that Jesus performed His first public miracle. Her powerful intercession is highlighted at Cana as she recognizes the steward's need and intercedes on his behalf, directing the servants to "do whatever he tells you." So it is with all of her spiritual children. Her intercession never fails and is always in perfect accord with the will of God.

- We pray for our children that if they are called to the vocation of Holy Matrimony they find holy spouses.

- Jesus is the invited guest of a marriage feast and provides the best wine for the bride and groom to enjoy. When we invite Jesus into our marriages he promises to provide for us the best wine, which is Himself, so that our marriages and families will be blessed with His saving graces.

- The Book of Revelation describes God's covenant with mankind in marital terms. He is the Bridegroom and we, His Church, are His Bride. He becomes intimately bonded to us as a husband and wife are bonded in love. Therefore, appropriately, Jesus begins to reveal His hidden, divine nature by performing His first miracle at a marriage banquet.

- We pray for the teachers of our children that they may convey to them the holiness of Christian marriage.

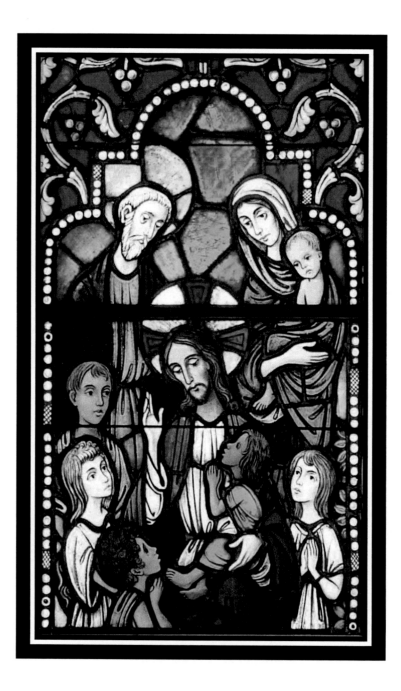

The Proclamation of the Kingdom

- "And I tell you, you are Peter, and on this rock I will build my church, and the powers of death shall not prevail against it. I will give you the keys of the kingdom of heaven, and whatever you bind on earth shall be bound in heaven..." (Matthew 16:18-19). Christ's Church is His kingdom on earth. The keys of the kingdom were an Old Testament symbol of authority given by the king to a trusted official to govern the kingdom. Christ gave the keys to Peter installing him with His authority as His first prime minister, first vicar, and first pope over His Kingdom on earth. The Good News is the proclamation of Christ's kingdom, a kingdom built on Peter, the Rock.

- We pray for our children who are called to the priesthood or religious life that we may encourage and strengthen them in choosing the holiest of all spouses, our Lord and Savior.

- Jesus announces to his fellow Jews that the Kingdom is at hand. All that God has prepared them for is about to be accomplished. And yet, somehow, most of God's chosen people at the time reject the message, as well as the Messenger. We pray that we always yearn for Jesus to be our King and His Kingdom to be our home.

- Jesus invites all who accept His message to become a part of His Kingdom. This message reveals the love between Jesus and the Father, a message which speaks to the life of that love. Although hidden in this age, His Kingdom is very much present to all who keep His commandments and do the will of the Father.

- We pray for the teachers of our children that they may impart a zeal for the Gospel in our children and that they may always encourage them in word and deed to actively engage in building the Kingdom.

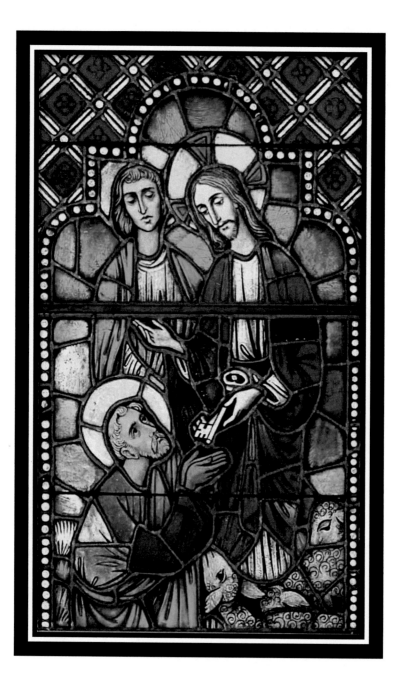

The Transfiguration

- "...Jesus took with him Peter and James and John, and led them up a high mountain apart by themselves; and he was transfigured before them, and his garments became glistening, intensely white.... And a cloud overshadowed them, and a voice came out of the cloud, 'This is my beloved Son; listen to him'" (Mark 9:2-3, 7). The grace we receive at Confirmation enables us to fulfill the mission of proclaiming the Good News. Help us to utilize the gifts of the Holy Spirit poured out on us at Confirmation to effectively witness for Christ.

- We pray for our children that every day they may be more and more transformed into the image of Christ.

- During the Transfiguration, Jesus lowers the veil momentarily to expose His glory. It must have been very hard to believe that Jesus was actually God, for He looked like an ordinary man. By faith we believe that He is God. By faith we believe that we have been given the divine life of God at baptism and by faith we believe that our world has been conquered by Christ and renewed. But at times this belief is challenging and hard. And our faith is weak. The Transfiguration is a gift given to us to strengthen our faith in a loving God whose glory and presence is very real even if it remains at times, here on earth, imperceptible.

- Jesus' closest friends, Peter, James and John, witness His Transfiguration and then later were asked to pray and keep watch with Him in the Garden during His Agony. These beloved friends were all aglow and eager to share in the glory of Christ on the mountaintop, but they slept when Jesus needed their support the most. Lord, we pray that we may readily share in the dark, sad moments of our friends as well as the happy, glorious ones.

- We pray for the teachers of our children that they will give our children insight into the glory of our Lord and His Kingdom.

31

The Institution of the Holy Eucharist

- The great Sacrament of Love and Life is the Eucharist where Jesus sacrifices Himself for His beloved Spouse. And we are His spouse! Women possess the unique understanding as to what it is to be open to life within the context of love and how to nurture that life to its fullest potential. Help us Mary to be fertile ground for all the graces Jesus desires to give us so that He may bring forth new life in us.

- We pray for our children that they will always stay close to you, Lord, in the Holy Eucharist so that you will always abide in them and they in you.

- Jesus gives us the gift of Himself in the Holy Eucharist. We are called to have the faith that it truly is Jesus when all we see and taste is bread and wine. But all He asks of us is to trust Him, and we do that by believing in His word and teachings that have been passed down to us by His Church. Help us Mary to persevere in faith and to turn to the Holy Eucharist often so that Jesus can renew our faith.

- The Passover feast is elevated by the One who celebrated it with Himself as both Priest and Victim. Then Jesus entered the eternal Holy of Holies, that is Heaven, with His Blood to offer it to the Father, thereby making His sacrifice eternal. At every Mass we partake in that eternal offering of the Son to the Father by means of the Eucharist. Help us Blessed Mother to appreciate the great gift of the Eucharist.

- We pray that the teachers of our children will grow in their devotion to the Holy Eucharist and show their love for the Holy Eucharist to our children.

THE SORROWFUL MYSTERIES

The Agony in the Garden

- "And he withdrew...knelt down and prayed, 'Father, if thou art willing, remove this cup from me; nevertheless not my will, but thine, be done.' And there appeared to him an angel from heaven, strengthening him" (Luke 22:41-43). We pray for our children that they may develop a fervent prayer life to prepare them for all their future sufferings.

- Like Adam, Jesus is tested in a garden. Adam's garden was paradise and yet he rejected God. Jesus is tested at the Mount of Olives and His time in the garden is filled with agony, yet even in all His agony he submits to the will of God. Help us Lord to do the same, to always choose to carry out the will of the Father no matter how difficult the circumstances.

- Dear Blessed Mother, when we are struggling with our children, questioning to know what is best, help us to always turn, with confidence, to prayer so you can strengthen and guide us. We should pray to do God's will no matter how difficult it may be, just as Jesus prayed in all His anguish the night before He was crucified.

- Jesus, being fully human like us, had the natural fear of suffering. But in His anguish He turned to prayer to be strengthened, so that He could fulfill the will of God. Prepare us Mary for our own personal sufferings, those which we face daily, but most of all those sufferings which really test our faith, so that like Christ we may accept them with love and patience.

- As Jesus suffered in the Garden, He prayed and the Father sent an angel to comfort and strengthen Him. God sends us angels also to help us live out our lives in obedience to His will. Remind us dear Blessed Mother to seek the aid of angels often, especially our guardian angels and our children's guardian angels. We cannot always be at our children's side through life, but their guardian angels never leave them.

The Scourging at the Pillar

- "So Pilate, wishing to satisfy the crowd, released for them Barabbas; and having scourged Jesus, he delivered him to be crucified" (Mark 15:15). We pray for our children that they may endure with patience their future sufferings, whether in mind or body.

- We are healed by His stripes, so it was prophesied in Isaiah 53. In order to heal us, Jesus had to undergo the brutal torture of scourging. Although it is easier to concentrate on the resurrection instead of the passion of Christ, it is the passion that heals us and it is only through the cross that we reach our resurrection.

- Help us Lord to have a spirit of mortification. Lord, you chose a life of poverty. We have been blessed by you with a life of abundance. By frequently self-sacrificing, for example by fasting or giving up luxuries, we strengthen our souls so that if we are ever stripped of these God-given blessings, we will remain strong in spirit and ever-faithful to You, our Lord.

- Jesus answered Pilate that His Kingdom was not of this world, but it is in the world, visibly present in His Church. If the Church is the Body of Christ and we are all part of that one Body through the Eucharist, then we can expect to be persecuted and ridiculed like Jesus as we hold fast to the teachings of His Church, His Kingdom here on earth.

- Jesus was accused and punished for a crime He did not commit. Saying nothing, He proceeded to pay a debt He didn't owe because we owed a debt we couldn't pay. Now He has given us His divine life so we too can endure the sufferings of our own passions in life. Help us Mary to teach our children to face and patiently endure sufferings out of love and obedience to the Father.

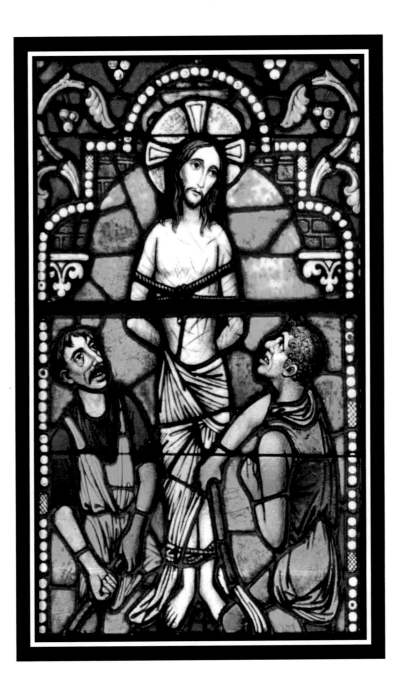

The Crowning With Thorns

- "And they clothed him in a purple cloak, and plaiting a crown of thorns they put it on him. And they began to salute him, 'Hail, King of the Jews!' And they struck his head with a reed, and spat upon him..." (Mark 15:17-19). We pray for our children that they have the moral courage to remain faithful to Christ in the face of persecutions for being children of the King.

- The Crowning with Thorns reveals the dreadful, fallen condition of our world. The King of Kings, the creator of the cosmos, is indeed crowned king by this world, but with a crown of thorns; the true King is humiliated and treated with disdain. Still, He is our King, and when we look upon Him bearing the crown of thorns we adore him and we worship him all the more.

- Needle-sharp thorns were heavily pressed in our Lord's most sacred head. Help us to have a spirit of moral courage and to teach our children not to care what other people think but always to do what is right, no matter the consequences, always to tell the truth and forever to live in the truth of Christ.

- Jesus, the King of Kings, endured all the mocking and humiliation which the crown of thorns symbolized. As children of the King, we too must endure in order to receive our inheritance. We pray that we and our children do not succumb to the pressures of this world but rather remain pure and chaste so as to faithfully live out the moral Law of God.

- Jesus Christ our Lord and King was mocked with the crown of thorns by His own subjects. This world hates righteousness and holiness and we too will be mocked if these virtues are seen in us. Help us Mary to stand upright as we live our lives in accordance with who we truly are: children of the King! May we always be proud to wear the crown of Jesus; for if we endure and share the crown of thorns in this life, we are promised to share in His crown of glory for all eternity.

The Carrying of the Cross

- "And as they led him away, they seized one Simon of Cyrene...and laid on him the cross, to carry it behind Jesus" (Luke 23:26). We pray for our children that they may have the strength to carry their crosses throughout their lives and that they may have the humility to ask for help when they need it.

- Jesus accepted help from a stranger as He carried the cross on the way to Calvary as if to give us the message that we are meant to help each other carry our crosses. Simon most likely didn't realize the treasure of graces attached to the job of helping his Lord with the cross; nor is it usually evident to us the blessings which we receive not only from accepting our own crosses but also from helping others with the burden of their crosses. Jesus in His humility allowed Simon to help Him; may we also allow others to help us.

- The cross, heavily burdened with the sins of the world, caused our Lord to fall three times. Each time He struggled to His feet and persevered. Help us Lord to never give up, to continue on after we fail and after we have sinned. Let us always remind our children that, no matter what, nothing they can do or say is beyond forgiveness and that we will always be there for them, to pick them up, to help them continue in life.

- Christ stumbled three times as He carried the cross. Mary was there to give Him the courage to continue. She is likewise always at our side, not to remove the crosses in our lives but to give us the strength and courage to overcome them.

- After the Sacrament of Confirmation, our children must be prepared to carry their crosses and witness to the world. They will be tested. Help us to prepare them well by reminding them to tap into the graces Jesus provides through His Sacraments, especially the Sacrament of Reconciliation which gives all of us the grace we need to overcome specifically those sins which cause us to trip and fall most often.

The Crucifixion and Death of Jesus

- "Then Jesus, crying with a loud voice, said, 'Father, into thy hands I commit my spirit!' And having said this he breathed his last" (Luke 23:46). We pray for our children that they may have a holy death.

- Jesus is now our High Priest, and He entered once for all into the perfect Holy of Holies, not made of this creation, but the heavenly one. He entered Heaven taking His own Blood thus securing an eternal redemption. When we lift up our hearts at every Mass we too enter into the Heavenly Place along with the angels and saints where for all eternity we find Jesus offering Himself to the Father.

- There is no greater love than to lay down your life for your friends. Jesus did this for us. We are all called to share in this divine love, a love which is self-giving. Mary, help us understand that when we live out our vocations as mothers, when we sacrifice and suffer for the sake of our children, the divine love within us increases and draws us closer to our Lord.

- Jesus is the perfect bridegroom who, on the cross, gives all His love and life to His bride. His bride, embodied in the Blessed Virgin Mary, then becomes the fruitful mother of all Christians, the Church. Help us, Mary, to be open to all the life-giving graces that Jesus offers us so that we too may be fruitful mothers who are always ready to share the love of Jesus.

- Before giving us the ultimate gift of His life on the cross, Jesus gave us His Mother. Apart from His own life, she was Jesus' most precious and beloved gift. Therefore, He chose to give her to us right before He gave us the gift of His life. The Father gave us His Son and the Son gave us His Mother. Help us to appreciate this love by treasuring the gift of your beloved mother; as St. John did, let us take Mary into our homes, our families, and our hearts.

THE GLORIOUS MYSTERIES

The Resurrection

- All of Jesus' promises are fulfilled in the Resurrection. If we believe and hope that someday we will be resurrected, then anything in this life can be endured. Help us Mary to instill this faith in our children, that they may never despair or lose hope in Christ.
- Jesus is the once-for-all perfect sacrifice and offering to the Father. He is eternally presenting Himself as the unblemished Lamb before the Father on our behalf. Therefore, we are filled with hope in the midst of all the sufferings and sin of this world and know that, through the merits of Christ, we can be perfected by the Holy Spirit and thereby call Heaven our home.
- "We were buried therefore with [Christ] by baptism into death, so that as Christ was raised from the dead by the glory of the Father, we too might walk in newness of life" (Romans 6:4). We pray for our children that they will live their lives worthy of the promises of the resurrection.
- St. Paul tells us in his Letter to the Romans that in Baptism we die and are buried with Christ and then rise from the font to live a resurrected life. Our lives and bodies now are not what they will be after our death but our souls are resurrected now with the life of the Spirit. We are now members of the Holy Trinity, the family of God. We are reminded of this truth every time we sign ourselves with the cross, doing everything in the name of the Father, Son and Holy Spirit.
- Dear Blessed Mother, it is so easy for us as mothers to be distracted with all the little problems of the day. Help us always to hold the bigger picture in our hearts and minds, to let go of the daily annoyances and to allow God to guide us in living our lives serving our families. Help us to make our homes happy, peaceful environments in which Christianity thrives in the security of Our Lord's promise of the resurrection.

The Ascension

- Before He ascended into Heaven, Jesus founded His Church as the means through which He would remain with us until the end of time, and through which He would continue to teach and guide and sanctify mankind until the end of the world. Help us Mary to teach our children to treasure the wonderful gift of Christ's Church.

- Jesus ascended into Heaven leaving the Apostles with His promise that the Holy Spirit would be sent. Without the Holy Spirit, we would be unable to partake in Christ's redemption. The Holy Spirit applies Christ's redemption to each one of us, giving us His divine life and nurturing us through the Eucharist with the very Body and Blood of Jesus. Help us Mary to teach our children of the vital, life-giving role of the Holy Spirit.

- We pray that our children may be a fragrant offering to the Father cloaked in the mantle of Our Lady at the hour of death.

- Jesus tells Mary Magdalene not to hold on to Him because He has not yet ascended to the Father. He still needs to enter the Heavenly Holy of Holies with his Blood procuring an eternal sacrifice, one that we enter into every time we enter the sanctuary at Mass. It is there that we join Jesus in the Holy of Holies where He is offering His Blood to the Father on our behalf continually. And it is at Mass where we join ourselves to Him in this holy unblemished offering.

- Dear Mother Mary, you must have so yearned to go with Jesus as He ascended into Heaven. Your life as the mother of the Redeemer was bathed in mysteries and yet you held these many mysteries in your heart with complete trust in the Father. Help us now, dear Mother, to trust more fully in God our Father that He will care for all our needs even in times when He seems distant because we know that it is in those moments when our faith will grow.

The Descent of the Holy Spirit at Pentecost

- Jesus sent the Holy Spirit to Mary and the Apostles on that Pentecost Sunday to give them courage and wisdom to go out and preach the Good News. Let us pray often to the Holy Spirit to help us teach our children to know God, by obeying His commandments, to love God, by loving one another, and to serve God, by spreading the Gospel and defending the Faith. Dwell within us, Holy Spirit, so that we may be shining examples to our children and to the world.

- Christ sent the Holy Spirit to give life to His newly formed Church. The Holy Spirit is the soul of the Mystical Body, the Church, and we are her members. Protect our families, Holy Spirit, which are domestic churches and are meant to image your Holy Church. We ask that you become the soul of our families so that every day we may grow in holiness.

- We pray for our children that they may be inspired by the Holy Spirit to be ambassadors of Christ to the world.

- The Church is the family of God visible here on earth filled with the Holy Spirit and given to us as a means for which Jesus continues his ministry of healing, teaching and nourishing. We have been reborn through the Church, healed through the Church, and are nourished by the Church. The Church is our mother who takes care of our every need.

- The Holy Spirit first descends on Mary at the Annunciation as she becomes the Mother of our Savior, Jesus Christ. Then the Holy Spirit descends on Jesus at His baptism as He begins His public ministry and the building of the kingdom of Heaven, the Church. The progression continues as the Holy Spirit descends on this newly formed Church with Mary, now the mother of all Christians, in the midst of them.

The Assumption of the Blessed Mother into Heaven

- What a privilege God bestowed on Mary as He assumed her sinless body and soul into Heaven to be reunited to her beloved Son. Jesus must have so loved her, as only a perfect son could love his mother. May we instill in our children the loving devotion that our Blessed Mother deserves. In return, we can be assured that she will always be with us, especially at the hour of our death.

- The depth of our love for Mary reveals the depth of our love for Christ. Do we fly to her with all our needs? Do we revere her for what God has done through her? If we pray to her and ask for her assistance, she can help us be more like her: a humble, loving, all-sacrificing mother.

- We pray for our children that they may always have a devotion to the holy rosary.

- What a mystery it is to ponder: that God the Son created His own mother and desired to redeem us through His Incarnation, by entering the womb of the Blessed Virgin Mary. By His design He chose to be bodily one with Mary His mother for nine months and to be nourished at her breasts. How fortunate we are to be mothers that through our children we are given a special insight into the intimacy that Mary and Jesus shared.

- Jesus could no longer be without His mother as His love for her bore her up to Heaven, body and soul. At the Annunciation, Mary was the first to accept the Word into her heart. By mothering Jesus, she became united to Him physically as He dwelt in her womb and nursed at her breast. Now at the Assumption she is the first Christian to be fully united body and soul to the glorified Jesus. Her reality is our promise if we remain faithful. May we pray to Mary often to help us as mothers to follow her into the loving embrace of our Lord, Jesus Christ.

The Coronation of Mary Queen of Heaven and Earth

- We pray that we always trust in Mary's intercession, for she will only lead us closer to Jesus. She is our advocate and our loving mother – she will never fail to help us. She will be our perfect guide and teacher in this life. No one knows better than Mary what we as mothers need to do, how we need to change, and what we must endure and suffer in order to reach our ultimate home.

- The most perfect person God ever created or will create is Mary. She is placed and honored and exalted over every other human person, over any king or national leader or power of the earth, over all creation. The single most important human person of all time is a woman, a humble handmaid, a mother. And because of Mary's humility, she has been elevated above all other creatures, by God, to be His Queen over all heaven and earth.

- We pray for our children that they may always see Mary as their true mother and trust her heavenly, queenly intercession.

- Mary is the Queen Mother who sits at her Son's right hand. The mother that He alone claimed while walking on this earth has now been given to us to be our mother. We are God's royal children. May we often remind our children of the dignity of being children of God and how blessed we all are to share in the banquet of the Lamb as we gather around the family table at every Mass.

- Because of Mary's humility she was seen by God to be full of grace and the perfect choice for the mother of His Son. Mary remained faithful to the Father's will all her life and therefore was crowned Queen over all creation. Help us, dear Blessed Mother, to always remain faithful in living out our vocations as mothers, to nurture the physical as well as the spiritual lives of our children.

How To Pray

The Stations Of The Cross

  This devotion was added to the Mothers' Rosary shortly after the prayer group formed. We pray the Stations of the Cross following the rosary during Lent. We pray it as a group beginning and ending the devotion with the Sign of the Cross. The leader announces the first station and everyone genuflects. The leader reads the first half of the station prayer and the group reads the second half of the station prayer (in bold italic print). The leader then reads the first part of each station's reflection, which is from the Blessed Mother's viewpoint, and the group reads the second part of the reflection, which is a mother's prayer (in bold print). Then everyone walks to the next station and repeats the steps.

1) Sign of the Cross

2) Announce the station

3) Genuflect

4) Station prayer: *We adore You, O Christ, and we praise You,* **because by Your holy cross You have redeemed the world.**

5) Station reflection

6) Proceed to next station

7) Repeat steps 2-6 until the 14th station is completed

8) Sign of the Cross

THE STATIONS OF THE CROSS

A Mother's Walk With Her Son

THE FIRST STATION: Jesus is Condemned to Death

We adore You, O Christ, and we praise You, **because by Your holy cross You have redeemed the world.**

It is early Friday morning; outside the Praetorium I hear the declaration that my Son has been condemned to death. The "hour" has come. I knew it would, but still I am terrified. Will I have the strength to walk with my Son in His darkest hour? Will I have the discipline to watch my innocent Son abused, condemned and killed by those He loves, those He is dying to help? I want to explain to them what they are doing. I want to make it all okay. Yet, in my heart I know that only my Son can truly make it all okay. I will remain silent as He is silent. I will accept as He accepts. I will unite my anguish with His. I will be one with Him in prayer as we walk this "hour" together.

Help me Mary to see my own sinfulness. I am the one who should be condemned, not your innocent Son. Jesus did this for me so that I may live. Help me never to forget this truth as I try to teach it to my children. Like you, Mary, I pray that I will have the strength to walk with my children, especially during their dark hours, to let them know that they are not alone, that they have dignity and are loved, and that all our sufferings when united to the sufferings of Jesus have great value and purpose.

THE SECOND STATION: Jesus Takes up His Cross

We adore You, O Christ, and we praise You, **because by Your holy cross You have redeemed the world.**

The heavy cross, laden with all the sins of the world, is heaved on the back of my Son, forcing Him to gasp for air as He stumbles forward. The guards are laughing and spitting at Him. They do not know that this is their King, this is their Savior. If they did know, would they care? I want to reason with them, but instead, I am to love them as my Son loves them, unconditionally. He will make all things new. I must bear the heaviness of the cross in my heart as I see my Son struggle forward on the rocky road.

Help me Mary to take up my cross every day and follow your Son. May my actions show my children the Christian way. I pray that I have the courage of Mary to watch my children take up their crosses and walk the road to Calvary. I want to take each cross from them and carry it myself, but I cannot. They will grow in holiness only if they carry it themselves. But, following Mary's example, I can pray for them as they bear their burden and I can carry their cross in my heart.

THE THIRD STATION: Jesus Falls the First Time

We adore You, O Christ, and we praise You, **because by Your holy cross You have redeemed the world.**

I watch as my Son trips and falls on the hard stony ground with the heavy cross crushing down on Him. I begin to tremble, as I wonder, is He already dead? His body is hardly recognizable. The guards kick Him and whip Him as He slowly moves to His feet to continue. My desire to take the cross and carry it myself is great; but my desire to see all mankind redeemed through my Son's suffering is greater. I must swallow the pain in my heart, have faith in the Father's will and silently pray with my Son as together we again move along the road to Calvary.

Help me Mary to rise up after I fall, after I sin. Help me to remember that you are there at my side praying for me that I will have the endurance and patience to continue on my road to Calvary. I pray that my children know that I too am there by their sides supporting them, especially when they fall. Like Mary, I am not there to remove their crosses; rather I am there to stand by my children's side to support, encourage, and pray that they will succeed in fulfilling the will of the Father.

THE FOURTH STATION: Jesus Meets His Mother

We adore You, O Christ, and we praise You, **because by Your holy cross You have redeemed the world.**

There is a break in the crowd and I am able to reach my Son. A touch, a word, a look is all I want, to let Him know that I am here with Him. But then, He knows I am with Him; I know He knows that I love Him. Our eyes meet. His face is severely swollen and bloodied, but still I can see that His eyes are full of love, those same eyes that gazed up at me when I held Him as a newborn infant in my arms for the first time. I wish I could hold Him again in my arms and protect Him. But then, it was for this very hour for which I protected Him all those many years. The words, "I love you," choke in my throat but even so, I can see through my tears that they still give Him the strength He was looking for.

There are moments when there is little I can do to help my children. It was so easy when they were young. I could solve all their little problems. But as adults they have to live their lives in a world which is entangled with big problems. And yet, a mother's heart united in prayer with the Immaculate Heart of Mary will always sustain her children along the road to Calvary. Help me Mary to more closely unite my heart with yours.

THE FIFTH STATION: Simon of Cyrene Helps Jesus Carry His Cross

We adore You, O Christ, and we praise You, **because by Your holy cross You have redeemed the world.**

As I watch my Son bow down closer and closer to the ground under the weight of the heavy cross, I wonder if He has the physical strength to carry it to the end. He is still moving forward, though His steps are now small and I see His legs shake and His knees begin to buckle. As I pray, "all is in the hands of God," the guards pull a strong-looking man named Simon from the crowd and order him to help Jesus carry the cross. Simon initially feels afflicted and those around him pity him; but I know differently. I know that Simon is privileged to have been chosen and will now receive blessings beyond measure in standing with my Son, in aiding Him in His physical weakness, in bearing some of the whippings directed toward my Son, in helping my Son fulfill His mission to redeem the world. For this, I will forever hold you close to my heart, Simon of Cyrene.

Dear Blessed Mother, help me to always remember and hold close to my heart those who help my children. As my children grow, my ability to help them turns from the physical to the spiritual. I always have the ability to pray that my children possess the humility to see that there are times when they need help from others and to accept it graciously. God bless all those who help my children today and may my children realize the blessings that come when they selflessly serve others.

THE SIXTH STATION: Veronica Wipes the Face of Jesus

We adore You, O Christ, and we praise You, **because by Your holy cross You have redeemed the world.**

Jesus, now with the help of Simon, is able to continue forward to the hill of crucifixion. But now I see my Son struggling as His most sacred blood flows continuously into His eyes from the sharp crown of thorns that pierces His brow. Suddenly, a woman forces her way through the crowd carrying a clean white cloth. She stops before Jesus and, oh so gently, presses the cloth to Jesus' face. This sweet act of kindness brings a spark of joy to our hearts, lifts our spirits, and fortifies us for the rest of our journey.

Dear Mother, this simple act of kindness was Veronica's gift to you in contrast to the cruel crown of thorns placed on your Son's head by the soldiers. I know I have added to the pain of those thorns by my sharp tongue, my sarcastic comments, my insensitive gossip. May your Son forgive me. Help me to be more like Veronica and always respond to the needs of others, in a kind, healing and nurturing manner. May I serve your Son with a mother's heart and, in doing so, bring joy to both you and to Him.

THE SEVENTH STATION: Jesus Falls the Second Time

We adore You, O Christ, and we praise You, **because by Your holy cross You have redeemed the world.**

JESUS FALLS THE SECOND TIME

My Son is visibly struggling as He tries to continue. The weight of the cross is bearing down hard on Him despite Simon's help. I notice that the crossbeam is digging into my Son's shoulder. Then I see Him fall again to the ground. The beam crushes His arm, that same sweet arm that wrapped my neck when I cradled Him as a babe in my arms. I wonder, how will He rise up, how will He continue on? The lash strikes again causing my Son to bleed all the more, causing my heart to pain all the more. He rises with the help of Simon. As He continues the walk to Calvary, I continue my prayer that I may be perfectly one with my Son through His passion; as I pray, Jesus glances my way revealing His perfect love.

Help me Mary to trust as you trusted so that I may possess the serenity and calm that you had as a result of your perfect faith in God and His holy will. So often I lose my calm when things don't go my way. I am impatient and wonder why God won't change things for the better more quickly. Help me Mary to have your complete trust that all is in the hands of God and that He knows infinitely better than I what my children need and when they need it.

THE EIGHTH STATION: Jesus Speaks to the Women of Jerusalem

We adore You, O Christ, and we praise You, **because by Your holy cross You have redeemed the world.**

I see my Son stop to speak to some women who have gathered before Him. They pity Him. Their pity, however, is so misguided for Jesus is doing the will of the Father; He is the remedy. And yet, my Son sees that there is maternal love behind their pity and cannot resist, despite His agony, to stop and preach one more sermon. He wants to help them see their own sinfulness before it is too late. I pray and hope that His words will not be wasted and that these women will follow Jesus.

Mary, despite all the agony your heart was suffering, you still prayed for these women. You did not resent their pity as I would have been so tempted to do. Help me Mary to always see the good in people and not to judge their motives or intentions. Help me to be patient especially to those people that I find difficult to be around, to those I would rather not bother with, and to those I find irritating. Help me to love all the people in my life with the love of Christ.

THE NINTH STATION: Jesus Falls the Third Time

We adore You, O Christ, and we praise You, **because by Your holy cross You have redeemed the world.**

Jesus is now almost at the hill of crucifixion. But, once again, I see Him trip and fall. His precious head hits the stony ground. The pain in my heart intensifies. My own legs feel weak as I want to rush to Him and cradle His head in my embrace. I want to kiss every precious wound on His body, as I did when He was a little boy after falling down and skinning His knee. Instead, the sound of the whips causes me to tremble as I watch my Son struggle to His feet. He continues. He will not give up because He loves us all with His infinite love. His strength becomes my own as I unite my heart all the more with His.

Mary, I cannot imagine the pain that you and your Son endured for love of me. I am so unworthy of this love, and yet, He calls me to love Him as He loves me, with an intimate love, a spousal love. When my cross bears down heavy on me, may I always look to your Son and remember the love He has for me. I pray that He fill me with His strength as I learn to unite my heart more fully with His.

THE TENTH STATION: Jesus is Stripped of His Garments

We adore You, O Christ, and we praise You, **because by Your holy cross You have redeemed the world.**

We have finally reached the hill of crucifixion, the place where my Son will ultimately give His life for the world. He is not allowed to rest even a moment as the guards roughly remove His garments, causing His blood-clotted wounds to reopen. The pain ripples across His whole body. The tunic, the priestly garment that I sewed with love for Him myself, is tossed aside as others argue over it. Stripping Him naked is a new humiliation that my Son must bear, but I know there is no other way. He endures all with love.

Mary, you never left Jesus' side. You bore all the humiliation with your Son. This world can be so cruel, and I have not been guiltless in this cruelty. How often have I laughed at or humiliated others with my actions or my words? I have made many mistakes. And even though I would like to think that my children are perfect, I know they have made many mistakes as well. Every time I hurt others, I hurt Jesus. I have done my share in humiliating your Son, Mary. Please forgive me.

THE ELEVENTH STATION: Jesus is Nailed to the Cross

We adore You, O Christ, and we praise You, **because by Your holy cross You have redeemed the world.**

My gentle Son willingly allows the soldiers to stretch out his arms and drive nails into them. This most cruel form of execution is how my Son will give His life out of love for His bride, for me and for you and for all who will accept and love Him. He opens His arms as if to say, I embrace the world; but then I hear the pounding of the iron and understand the explosion going off in His head. His body is pierced as is my soul. His pain is torturous, but His love is even greater and my heart is all the more united to His. I watch them hoist the cross into the ground jarring my Son's body. There He is, my Son, this world's creator and savior. All I can do now is pray and give Him my loving support as He struggles for every breath.

There are times when my children are suffering and all I can do as a mother is give my loving support and intercessory prayer. During these trials and difficult times, remind me Mary that my love and prayer are the most powerful weapons a mother possesses against the evil that seeks to destroy her children. Increase my faith, so that I may see that when I lovingly support my family I follow in the footsteps of all the holy women in history who patterned their lives after you, Mary, who fully supported your Son during His passion.

THE TWELFTH STATION: Jesus Dies on the Cross

*We adore You, O Christ, and we praise You, **because by Your holy cross You have redeemed the world.***

The labor is now near the end, the delivery imminent. I stand with John, the faithful disciple, as my Son bows His head and gives His life to me, as a bridegroom does to his bride; He gives me to John to be the mother of all the disciples, all the children of God. I think back when I carried Jesus in my womb. I was filled with awe and wonder. Bringing Jesus into this world brought me no pain, only joy. But the pain of this labor and delivery, of bringing humanity into the kingdom of life, is great. Yet, I am still filled with awe and wonder as I pray to understand the deep mysteries of my God, my Lord, my Son.

Mary, I see now how your Son is the perfect bridegroom to the end, giving His entire life to His bride, holding nothing back. Mary, you are now his fruitful bride, mother of us all. May I embrace you fully as my mother, for you possess the fullness of your Son's life and love. What a mystery, what a wonder. May I spend the rest of my life contemplating this love. And may I live my life as a wife and mother, modeling you, so that my family may be an example of this love to the world. Mary, I place my family under your maternal protection.

The Thirteenth Station: Jesus is Taken from the Cross

We adore You, O Christ, and we praise You, **because by Your holy cross You have redeemed the world.**

The wind is blowing and the ground is shaking as this world is in turmoil over the death of its creator, my Son. Jesus is taken off the cross and placed in my arms. I hold Him now at the end of His earthly life as I did when He first entered this world as the fruit of my womb. He was a perfect, precious infant. Now, I see clearly the effects of the world's sin on His body. His physical agony is over now. And yet, I cannot help but weep as I think of the irony of my Son who is Life itself, dead in my arms. I gave Him life at the beginning of this journey, and now He has given His life totally back to me so that my maternal fruitfulness may be complete. The pain in my heart is intense, yet I know that it is a heart fully united to my Son's most Sacred Heart.

What pain you endured, Mary, as you held your dearly beloved Son in your arms. My sin caused this agony for both Him and you. And yet you both forgive me because you love me. Had I been the only person on earth, your Son still would have gone through all of this torture just for me. Mary, help me to love your Son. Teach me the way, for you know the way. Help me to succeed in being completely devoted and faithful to my maternal vocation. Help me to be more united to your heart by being more united to my spouse, so that our children may always see us as one. Bring the Holy Spirit into my marriage and into my home so that my family may more perfectly image the love of Christ.

THE FOURTEENTH STATION: Jesus is Placed in the Tomb

We adore You, O Christ, and we praise You, **because by Your holy cross You have redeemed the world.**

It is time to bury you, my Son. I am thankful that I am allowed to attend to your precious body with the burial cloths myself. You have now renewed every aspect of humanity, even death. I am buried with you in my heart, my Lord, my Son. And so it will be with every believer, buried with you in baptism, so that every faithful follower will be raised with you to new life. My earthly journey with you has reached its end, and yet we are now more united than ever. Though the pain in my heart remains, it is a pain worth bearing as I know from it much fruit will come. Until I am with you in glory I will endure this pain so that your life may spread through me to your infant Church, a Church that will continue to grow, revealing your everlasting glory.

Mary, teach me to be a mother conformed to your Son's holy will and a perfect conduit of His love for my family. Reduce me to nothing so that I may more readily spread His sacrificial love to my spouse, to my children and to all those in my life. I am so little, so helpless, but with God's grace, may I live my life here on earth helping others see the love of your Son, a love poured out from God the Father, a love burning with the desire of the Holy Spirit, and a love which bears the marks of your constant maternal protection and gentleness. Help me Mary to be a mother whose heart is united to your Immaculate Heart, so that I may be forever united to your Son's Sacred Heart.

MATER DOLOROSA

"Mater Dolorosa" is Latin for Sorrowful Mother. St. Madeleine Sophie Barat was known to have had a special devotion to Our Lady of Sorrows as she often reminded the religious of the Society: "Nothing is asked in vain of Our Lady of Sorrows; gratitude compels me to make this known." During a most stressful time for the Society in 1839, St. Madeleine Sophie consecrated the Society to Our Lady of Sorrows. The consecration prayer used by St. Madeleine Sophie was then repeated every year by the religious of the Sacred Heart and the Rosary of the Seven Sorrows became a common devotion recited on Fridays. September 15th is the feast day of Our Lady of Sorrows.

HOW TO PRAY THE ROSARY OF
THE SEVEN SORROWS OF MARY

This devotion is prayed on a rosary or chaplet made up of seven sets of seven beads, with each set separated by a medal usually depicting one of the seven sorrows. Our Mothers' Rosary group gathers around the side altar dedicated to Our Lady of Sorrows in the Villa Duchesne and Oak Hill School chapel. The leader reads each sorrow reflection which is from Mary's perspective and the group reads the corresponding sorrow prayer from a mother's perspective in bold print. The opening and closing prayers are also read by the group. Incorporated in the closing prayer are the words of St. Madeleine Sophie and Mother Janet Stuart, RSCJ (Superior General of the Society of the Sacred Heart 1911-1914) as our Mothers' Rosary group wishes to honor the Religious of the Sacred Heart who passed on this devotion to us.

1) Sign of the Cross

2) Opening prayer

3) Sorrow reflection

4) Sorrow prayer

5) Our Father

6) Seven Hail Marys

7) Repeat steps 3-6 until all seven sorrows are completed

8) Three Hail Marys in honor of the tears of Mary

9) Closing prayer

10) Sign of the Cross

THE ROSARY OF
THE SEVEN SORROWS
OF MARY

OPENING PRAYER

Mary, Mother of Sorrows, we begin this rosary in a prayer of thanksgiving for your motherly protection over us and for the many graces you have poured out on us and our families. Help us to bear the cross of Christ which is the cross of love, remembering His wounds, His piercings, and His death. Reveal to us, dear Mother, as we walk with you through these sufferings, the compassion of your Son's most Sacred Heart, and, through your Immaculate Heart, align our hearts more closely with His. Amen.

THE PROPHECY OF SIMEON

I believe that this man, Simeon, is holy and his words are true. He is preparing me for my future sufferings. It is so hard to believe this prophecy as I look down at my beautiful, innocent child. My answer is still, "yes," I will do the will of God, I will continue to be one with this child, this  Son who came from my body and who depends on me for nourishment. I will continue to nurture and safeguard this child for the hour that God wills, the hour that will pierce my soul through.

Mary, prepare us for all our future sufferings especially those that involve our children.

Our Father

Seven Hail Marys

THE FLIGHT INTO EGYPT

What panic I feel as Joseph tells me that we need to leave Bethlehem immediately, for we are in grave danger. Something bad is imminent, I can feel it as we leave under the cover of night. With each step away from our homeland toward Egypt I feel a bit more assured of safety. But then I hear it, the haunting sounds of crying women who have had their young children torn viciously from their arms. All I can do is weep bitterly for them as I cradle the sleeping Jesus closer to my sorrowful heart for this hour is not my Son's hour. I praise you God for the gift of Joseph, to whom we have been entrusted. For now, we are safe under his protection.

Mary, bless our husbands who model St. Joseph and protect and guard our families.

Our Father

Seven Hail Marys

THE LOSS OF JESUS IN THE TEMPLE

Traveling home to Nazareth in the company of our kin, Joseph and I suddenly realize that Jesus is missing. Together, we begin to anxiously search for our young Jesus. So many questions preoccupy our aching heads as our eyes frantically dart about hoping to see His face again. Did someone take  Him? Is this the hour? Is He still alive? Guilt and blame weigh heavily on my sorrowful heart as we begin the third day of our search. Joseph and I, holding hands, climb the stairs of the Jerusalem Temple to pray together when we catch sight of Jesus. His gaze falls on us and He reveals that His separation from us was necessary to fulfill the will of His Father.

Mary, bless my husband and me as we search for guidance, as we pray that God's will be done, and as we suffer together to bear spiritual fruit for the sake of each other and for our children.

Our Father

Seven Hail Marys

MARY MEETS JESUS ON THE WAY TO CALVARY

My sorrowful heart is breaking as I meet my Son on His way to the hill of crucifixion. This is it, the hour of which holy Simeon prophesied so many years ago. Indeed, my soul is being pierced, and yet I see only love in the eyes of Jesus. I won't leave Him now, though witnessing the cruelty of this world pressing down full force through the weight of the cross on my Son's back is nearly impossible for me to bear. He has one word for me, "courage." I have one word in reply, "yes." Thy will be done in all things.

Mary, in the dark days of suffering, give me courage that I may always say "yes" to God.

Our Father

Seven Hail Marys

JESUS DIES ON THE CROSS

My soul is now pierced through, for what greater suffering is there for a mother than to witness the death of her own dearly beloved son? "It is finished," His hour is complete, and yet my role not only continues but broadens as now I become the mother of the rest of my children, those who will follow His Way, those who have been brought to life through His death. I will continue to mother, and my sorrowful heart will enlarge as I witness the rest of my children endure their own sufferings. They will not be alone as I will always be with my children especially at the hour of their death.

Mary, help me to embrace my cross and follow Jesus all my life. Each day may I die more to myself and live more for others.

Our Father

Seven Hail Marys

MARY RECEIVES THE DEAD BODY OF JESUS

I receive my Son's body into my loving embrace one last time here on earth. He didn't deserve this; He owed us nothing, but then this is how true love is displayed. Love is not due, it is given out of pure self-sacrifice simply for the sake of the beloved. I love Him. I have always loved Him and I will continue to love Him through His Mystical Body as I embrace every Christian as my child, as a member of His Body, the Body that I conceived and became intimately one with in my womb. I will continue to love and nourish my Son's Body as I love and nourish every member of His Church.

Mary, hold me forever in your embrace as you held your Son. May I learn from you how to be a truly loving mother.

Our Father

Seven Hail Marys

JESUS IS LAID IN THE TOMB

I carefully attend to Jesus' body with the burial cloths myself. It is now that I can see the mark of every cruel lash and every piercing upon His flesh. Here He is, my Son, the Light of the World, being placed in a cold, dark tomb. But I know His Light has triumphed over the darkness, and through the Holy Spirit it  will spread to every corner of this darkened world.

Mary, show me how to be a worthy instrument of the Holy Spirit so that I may spread the Light of Christ to my family and to the world.

Our Father

Seven Hail Marys

Three Hail Marys in honor of the sorrowful tears shed by Mary

CLOSING PRAYER

Most Sorrowful Mother, "Love gave you the cross, grant that the cross may give us love."[1] Be with us, Mother, as we try to follow your Son along our road of salvation. Enlighten us so that we may come to understand that "in the spiritual life the fruit of sorrow is joy. When sorrow falls on the heart that loves God, it is sure to expand in that heart under the sunshine of faith and love, till it finally ripens into joy, whose fruit in turn becomes a seed for eternity."[2] May we learn to see the cross as a means of finding the love of Christ and thereby draw from it joy and peace. Amen.

---

[1] Taken from St. Madeleine Sophie's prayer to Our Lady of Sorrows.

[2] An excerpt from the writings of Mother Janet Stuart, RSCJ, during a conference in September 1911 on Our Lady of Sorrows.

FAVORITE PRAYERS

ST. GERARD PRAYERS (Patron saint of expectant mothers)

A Prayer for Motherhood

O glorious St. Gerard, powerful intercessor before God, and wonder worker of our day, I call upon you and seek your help. You who always fulfilled God's will on earth, help me to do God's holy will. Intercede with the Giver of life, from whom all parenthood proceeds, that I may conceive and raise children who will please God in this life, and be heirs to the kingdom of heaven. Amen.

A Prayer for a Mother with Child

O Almighty and Everlasting God, Who, through the operation of the Holy Spirit, did prepare the body and soul of the glorious Virgin Mary to be a worthy dwelling place of Thy Divine Son; and, through the operation of the same Holy Spirit, did sanctify St. John the Baptist, while still in his mother's womb; hearken to the prayers of Thy humble servant who implores Thee, through the intercession of St. Gerard, to protect me amid the dangers of child-bearing and to watch over the child with which Thou hast deigned to bless me; that it may be cleansed by the saving water of Baptism and, after a Christian life on earth, it may with its mother attain everlasting bliss in Heaven. Amen.

MORNING OFFERING

O Jesus, through the Immaculate Heart of Mary, I offer You all my prayers, works, joys and sufferings of this day, in union with the Holy Sacrifice of the Mass throughout the world, for all the intentions of Your Sacred Heart and of the Immaculate Heart of Your mother Mary, for the conversion and salvation of sinners, in reparation and atonement for sins, for the poor souls in purgatory and for the intentions of our Holy Father, the Pope. Amen.

PRAYER FOR THE UNBORN

Jesus, Mary, and Joseph, I love you very much. I beg you to spare the life of the unborn child I have spiritually adopted who is in danger of abortion. Amen.

THE MEMORARE

Remember, O most gracious Virgin Mary, that never was it known that anyone who fled to thy protection, implored thy help, or sought thy intercession was left unaided. Inspired with this confidence, I fly to thee, O Virgin of virgins, my Mother; to thee do I come, before thee I stand, sinful and sorrowful. O Mother of the Word Incarnate, despise not my petitions, but in thy mercy hear and answer me. Amen.

THE PRAYER TO ST. JOSEPH

O St. Joseph, whose protection is so great, so strong, so prompt before the throne of God, I place in you all my interests and desires. O St. Joseph, do assist me by your powerful intercession and obtain for me from your Divine Son all spiritual blessings through Jesus Christ, Our Lord; so that having engaged here below your Heavenly power I may offer my thanksgiving and homage to the most loving of Fathers. O St. Joseph, I never weary contemplating you and Jesus asleep in your arms. I dare not approach while He reposes near your heart. Press Him in my name and kiss His fine head for me, and ask Him to return the kiss when I draw my dying breath. St. Joseph, patron of departing souls, pray for us. Amen.

PRAYERS TO MATER

Mother most admirable, guardian of the interior life, we ask you to loosen our grasp on visible things and help us to see the invisible which your eyes behold: the invisible life, the invisible action, the invisible love, all those realities of faith that are for us eternal values. When we get lost in the devouring activity of the visible and often not so important things, keep us in the light of the unseen and make us strong as though we beheld the invisible. Above and beyond accessory trifles that concern us and carry us away, that burden our minds and hearts and distort our scale of values, give us, we ask you, a hunger and thirst for the essential: the wish of the Lord and the work of his love to which he has called each of us. Amen.

-Mother Marie-Therese de Lescure, RSCJ

Mater, as I turn to you in prayer, I ask you to help me to love and long for a life of simplicity and to be open to God's Word in my life. Life is often hard. It is not easy to love everyone as Jesus did, to remain calm and at peace with the changes of life, to be humble when pride rises up within me. There are days when everything seems a burden, but you can make everything easier; not by taking away the hard things, for God did not take away yours. You make them easier by making our love stronger. It was love that impelled you to say that total and unconditional "yes" to God. That word, once given, you never took back. You never resisted suffering but opened yourself to its action. May your example be my strength. Help me to have a strong love. When my love grows weak, give me, your child, something of your own love that I may learn again from you what true love means. May I remember that you not only show me the way, but you walk the way with me, giving me at every step, the grace I need. Amen.

ST. THERESE OF THE LITTLE FLOWER NOVENA

St. Therese, the Little Flower, please pick me a rose from the heavenly garden and send it to me with a message of love. Ask God to grant me the favor I thee implore and tell Him I will love Him each day more and more.

Say the above prayer, plus 5 Our Father's, 5 Hail Mary's, and 5 Glory Be's on five consecutive days. On the fifth day, after the 5th set of prayers has been completed, offer one more set of 5 Our Father's, 5 Hail Mary's and 5 Glory Be's.

DAILY PRAYER OF ST. MADELEINE SOPHIE BARAT

O Sacred Heart of Jesus, give me a heart that is one with Your own; a humble heart that knows and loves its nothingness; a gentle heart that holds and calms its own anxieties; a loving heart that has compassion for the suffering of others; a pure heart that recoils even at the appearance of evil; a detached heart that longs for nothing other than the goodness of heaven; a heart detached from self-love and embraced by the love of God, its attention focused on God, its goodness is its only treasure in time and eternity. Amen.

A PRAYER OF ST. ROSE PHILIPPINE DUCHESNE

Lord, You alone are the Center in which I find rest.
Give me Your arm to support me,
Your shoulders to carry me,
Your breast to lean upon,
Your Cross to uphold me,
Your Body to nourish me.
In You, Lord, I sleep and rest in peace.

A PRAYER BEFORE STUDYING SACRED SCRIPTURE

O Holy Spirit of God, with St. Madeleine Sophie we pray, "If I had my life to live over again, I would live it in constant fidelity to the Holy Spirit." We open ourselves today to Your Word for us in the pages of the Sacred Scriptures. Reveal to us Your deepest desires for us. Fill us with courage and generosity to hear Your Word in the depths of our hearts, to ponder that Word with one another, and to give ourselves over, without reservation, to Your life-giving movement in us and in our world, a world so in need of healing and hope. We pray to You, in the communion of the Father and the Son forever and ever. Amen.

A PRAYER FOR THE ELECTION OF CIVIL SERVANTS

Lord Jesus Christ, You told us to give to Caesar what belongs to Caesar and to God what belongs to God. Enlighten the minds of our people in America. May we choose a President of the United States and other government officials according to Your Divine Will. Give our citizens the courage to choose leaders of our nation who respect the sanctity of unborn human life, the sanctity of marriage, the sanctity of marital relations, the sanctity of the family and the sanctity of the aging. Grant us the wisdom to give You what belongs to You, our God. If we do this as a nation, we are confident You will give us an abundance of Your blessings through our elected leaders. Amen.

-Fr. John Hardon, S.J.

In Gratitude

With a grateful heart, I thank my mother who prayed for me.
I love you, Mom.

I HAD A MOTHER WHO PRAYED FOR ME

I had a mother who prayed for me
She fell asleep at night with her rosary
And all those Hail Mary's and Glory Be's
Were sent heavenward for my siblings and me.

I had a mother who taught me to pray,
And every morning of every day,
She blessed me while sending me on my way,
And said prayers for me for the rest of the day.

Now I am a mother with kids of my own.
For years I have taught them the prayers I had known.
Now as I say my prayers all alone,
And most of my visits with my kids are by phone,
I pray that they each will find God on their own.

There are those who have tangible wealth untold,
All the world has to offer in silver and gold,
But richer than I they will never be,
I had a mother who prayed for me.

And my own dear children may not be kings,
Or queens with holdings and earthly things.
But surely they'll grow into good women and men,
They had a mother who prayed for them.

(author unknown)

THE AUTHOR

Polly and her husband of 33 years have 8 children. Polly, as well as her 8 children, attended Villa Duchesne and Oak Hill School. As a parent, she formed the Spirituality Committee of the Mothers' Club which helps to organize weekly Mass intentions, First Friday Eucharistic Adoration, Bible Study, and the weekly Mothers' Rosary. She remains active in the school, leads two Bible Study groups for parents, and can still be found praying the rosary weekly in the school chapel.

Made in the USA
San Bernardino, CA
05 November 2018